The Hidden World of Microorganisms

A High School Student's Guide to Microbiology

Dr. Anjana J.C & Sanath Nair

Dedication

To our amazing son,

This book is dedicated to you... We hope it sparks your imagination and feeds your hunger for knowledge about the tiny creatures that are all around us. We're sure each page will bring you one step closer to understanding the fascinating world of microbiology.

So keep exploring and discovering, our little scientist. We can't wait to see all the amazing things you'll achieve and how you'll change the world with your knowledge.

With all our love,

Anjana & Sanath

Content

Preface

Hey there, curious minds!

Welcome to "The Hidden World of Microorganisms - A High School Student's Guide to Microbiology" Are you fascinated by tiny creatures you can't even see with your naked eye? Do you want to learn about the role of microorganisms in our environment, human health, and society? Then this book is perfect for you!

We've designed this guide to provide you with a comprehensive understanding of microbiology, from microbial diversity and classification to the various applications of microorganisms in biotechnology. You'll learn about microbial metabolism and growth, genetics, and the role of microorganisms in causing infectious diseases.

But that's not all - we'll also explore the fascinating ways microorganisms interact with their environment, including their roles in biogeochemical cycles and symbiotic relationships. We'll discuss the applications of environmental microbiology and the ethical considerations associated with using microorganisms in biotechnology.

This book is written in a conversational tone that is easy to understand, even if you are new to microbiology. We hope that you'll find the information in this guide fascinating and inspiring and that it will encourage you to explore this exciting field further.

So, let's dive in and explore the fantastic world of microbiology together!

Introduction to Microbiology

Welcome to the world of microbiology! In this chapter, we will take a closer look at this fascinating field of study and explore the world of microorganisms.

So, what exactly is microbiology? Microbiology is the study of microorganisms - tiny living things too small to be seen with the naked eye. These organisms include bacteria, viruses, fungi, and protozoa. Despite their size, these tiny creatures play a crucial role in our world and lives.

Microorganisms are living things that are too small to see without the help of a microscope. They are found all around us, from the soil beneath our feet to the air we breathe. Some examples of microorganisms include bacteria, which can be found in various environments and play various roles in our world, and viruses, which cause various common illnesses.

Fungi are another type of microorganism, and they can be found in a wide range of environments, from the soil to our own bodies. Some fungi are used to make bread and beer, while others can cause infections in people with weakened immune systems.

Protozoa are another type of microorganism, and they can be found in water, soil, and other environments. Some protozoa are responsible for causing diseases such as malaria. In contrast, others are important in the nutrient cycling process in soil.

Despite their small size, microorganisms play a critical role in our world. Bacteria, for example, are involved in the process of decomposition, which helps to break down dead plant and animal material and return nutrients to the soil. They are also used to produce many common foods, such as yogurt and cheese.

Viruses, while often associated with illness, can also be beneficial. For example, bacteriophages are viruses that infect bacteria and can be used to control bacterial infections in animals and humans.

Fungi are important decomposers in the environment and are used in producing many different foods, such as bread, cheese, and soy sauce. Some fungi are also used in the production of antibiotics and other medicines.

Protozoa play an essential role in the nutrient cycling process in soil and can also be used as indicators of water quality.

As you can see, microorganisms are an incredibly diverse and influential group of organisms. By studying microbiology, we can better understand their roles in our world and how to use them to improve our lives.

Microorganisms are all around us and play various essential roles in our world. Let's examine some of these roles and how they impact our daily lives.

Nutrient cycling is one of the most critical processes in microorganisms. When plants and animals die, microorganisms break down their bodies, which release nutrients into the soil.

These nutrients are then available for other plants and animals to use, helping to support a healthy ecosystem.

Decomposition is another crucial process that microorganisms are involved. When organic matter decomposes, it releases carbon dioxide and other gases into the atmosphere, helping to regulate our planet's climate. Microorganisms also play a role in the breakdown of human waste, which helps prevent disease spread.

Fermentation is when microorganisms convert sugars into alcohol, acids, or gases. This process produces many common foods, such as yogurt, cheese, and bread. Fermentation also produces beer, wine, and other alcoholic beverages.

While many microorganisms are beneficial, some can cause diseases in humans and other animals. For example, bacteria such as Streptococcus and Staphylococcus can cause infections. In contrast, viruses such as the flu and the common cold can cause illness. These microorganisms can spread through the air, make contact with contaminated surfaces, or insect bites like mosquitoes.

On the other hand, some microorganisms are used to produce medicines and other healthcare products. Antibiotics, for example, are drugs made from certain types of bacteria and fungi. These drugs are used to treat bacterial infections and have saved countless lives.

In the food industry, microorganisms produce various products, such as cheese, yogurt, and bread. For example, the bacteria used to make yogurt convert lactose, a sugar found in milk, into lactic acid. This process gives yogurt its tangy flavour and helps preserve the milk.

As you can see, microorganisms play a vital role in our world, from supporting the growth of plants to producing life-saving medicines. By studying microbiology, we can better understand these tiny organisms and how they impact our daily lives.

The study of microbiology has a fascinating history that dates back centuries. In the 17th century, a Dutch scientist named Antonie van Leeuwenhoek was the first to observe microorganisms using a microscope that he had made himself. He discovered a new world of tiny creatures, including bacteria and protozoa. He described them in detail in his writings.

As technology advanced, so did our understanding of microorganisms. In the late 1800s, a scientist named Louis Pasteur conducted a series of experiments that helped to prove the germ theory of disease. He showed that microorganisms could cause infections and developed methods for sterilizing equipment and preventing the spread of disease.

In the 20th century, the field of microbiology exploded with new discoveries and breakthroughs. One of the most important discoveries was the development of antibiotics, first discovered in the 1920s. Antibiotics are drugs that can kill or inhibit the growth of bacteria. They have saved countless lives by treating infections that were once deadly.

Another major breakthrough in microbiology was the development of vaccines. Vaccines stimulate the immune system to recognize and fight off a particular disease. They have been used to prevent various illnesses, from polio to measles to the flu.

Microbiology has also played a crucial role in the field of agriculture. For example, Rhizobium bacteria can convert nitrogen gas from the air into a form that plants can use. This process, called nitrogen fixation, helps to fertilize the soil and improve crop yields. Microorganisms have also been used to develop new methods for controlling pests and diseases in crops.

Technological advances have allowed us to study microorganisms in even greater detail in recent years. For example, the development of DNA sequencing has enabled scientists to identify and study the genetic makeup of microorganisms. This has resulted in new discoveries about the relationships between various microorganism species and their interactions with their environments.

Overall, the study of microbiology has profoundly impacted our understanding of the world around us. By learning more about these tiny creatures, we can develop new treatments for diseases, improve crop yields, and better understand the natural world. It's an exciting field that will yield new discoveries and breakthroughs.

Now that you have a better understanding of microbiology let's take a closer look at some of the key concepts and topics you will encounter in this field of study. We will explore the different types of microorganisms, their structures and functions, their roles in human health and disease, and much more.

Whether you are a high school student interested in pursuing a career in microbiology or simply curious about the world around you, this book will provide a solid foundation in this exciting and ever-evolving field of study. So, let's dive in and discover the fascinating world of microorganisms together!

Microbial Diversity and Classification

Welcome to the fascinating world of microbiology! In this chapter, we'll be delving into microbial diversity and classification.

Let's start with the basics - what are microorganisms? They're tiny living creatures that are too small to be seen by the naked eye. Microorganisms come in many forms, from bacteria and fungi to protists and viruses. These tiny creatures play crucial roles in our lives, from helping us digest food to producing medicine and breaking down waste.

Microorganisms are truly unique creatures, and one thing that makes them so fascinating is their incredible diversity. Despite being so small, there are countless microorganisms, each with unique characteristics and abilities.

SHAPES OF BACTERIA

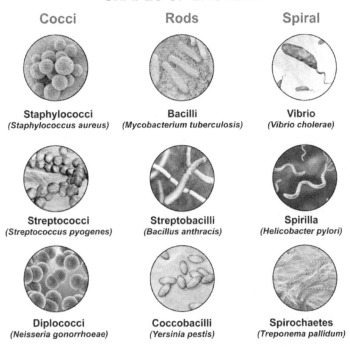

Cocci	Rods	Spiral
Staphylococci *(Staphylococcus aureus)*	**Bacilli** *(Mycobacterium tuberculosis)*	**Vibrio** *(Vibrio cholerae)*
Streptococci *(Streptococcus pyogenes)*	**Streptobacilli** *(Bacillus anthracis)*	**Spirilla** *(Helicobacter pylori)*
Diplococci *(Neisseria gonorrhoeae)*	**Coccobacilli** *(Yersinia pestis)*	**Spirochaetes** *(Treponema pallidum)*

Let's take a closer look at bacteria as an example. Bacteria come in all shapes and sizes, from spiral-shaped to rod-shaped and even spherical. Some bacteria have a thick outer layer called a capsule. In contrast, others have long, hair-like structures called flagella that they use to move around.

But the differences between bacteria don't just stop at their appearance. Some bacteria are aerobic, meaning they need oxygen to survive. In contrast, others are anaerobic and can only live in environments without oxygen. Some bacteria can survive in extreme environments, such as the hot springs in Yellowstone National Park, where the water temperature can reach 80°C!

In addition to their morphology, microorganisms differ in physiology and metabolism. Some microorganisms, like plants, are photosynthetic and can use light energy to produce food. For example, Cyanobacteria, also known as blue-green algae, are photosynthetic bacteria that play an essential role in the aquatic food chain.

Other microorganisms are chemosynthetic and use chemicals to survive. For example, some bacteria found in the deep ocean can use chemicals such as hydrogen sulfide to produce their food. These unique traits help us understand each microorganism's role in the environment and our lives.

By studying the diversity of microorganisms, we can gain insights into the processes that drive life on our planet. For example, the nitrogen cycle, essential for plant growth, relies on bacteria that can convert atmospheric nitrogen into a form that plants can use.

The world of microorganisms is incredibly diverse and complex, and it's exciting to think about all the different types of microorganisms that exist and their roles in our lives. From bacteria to fungi to protists and viruses, each microorganism has a story to tell. By studying them, we can gain a deeper appreciation for the complexity of life.

Now that we've explored the incredible diversity of microorganisms, you might be wondering how scientists classify and identify them. Well, there are several methods that scientists use, and each method gives us a different perspective on these tiny creatures.

One of the most potent tools for classifying microorganisms is genetic sequencing. This method involves reading the genetic code of a microorganism to determine its relationship to other organisms. By comparing the genetic code of different microorganisms, scientists can group them into different categories, such as bacteria, archaea, fungi, and protists.

Biochemical tests are another method that scientists use to identify microorganisms. These tests involve adding different substances to a sample of microorganisms and observing how they react. Scientists can determine what kind of microorganism they are dealing with based on their reaction. For example, a standard biochemical test is the Gram stain, which differentiates between two types of bacteria - Gram-positive and Gram-negative.

Microscopy is also a valuable tool for studying microorganisms. By looking at them under a microscope, scientists can observe their physical characteristics, such as shape, size, and movement. For example, suppose you looked at a bacteria sample under a microscope. In that case, you might see some bacteria that are rod-shaped and others that are spherical. These physical characteristics can be used to help identify different types of microorganisms.

Understanding microbial diversity and classification is essential for many reasons. For one thing, it helps us to better understand the world around us. Microorganisms play a vital role in the ecosystem. By understanding their relationships and interactions with other organisms, we can gain insights into the processes that drive life on our planet.

Furthermore, understanding microbial diversity can have practical applications in our daily lives. For example, scientists have discovered that some microorganisms can be used to produce biofuels. In contrast, others can help break down harmful environmental pollutants. By harnessing the unique abilities of different microorganisms, we can find new ways to improve our world.

While the world of microorganisms may seem small, it is incredibly complex and diverse. Scientists use various methods to classify and identify microorganisms. By understanding their relationships and interactions, we can gain a deeper appreciation for the complexity of life.

The world of microbiology is vast and endlessly fascinating. From the smallest bacteria to the most complex viruses, each microorganism has a story to tell. By exploring their diversity and classification, we can gain a deeper appreciation for the complexity of life and the incredible power of these tiny creatures. So let's continue our journey into the microbial world, and who knows what discoveries we may uncover next!

Microbial Metabolism and Growth

Welcome to the fascinating world of microbial metabolism and growth!

At first glance, you might think these tiny organisms are too small to have much happening inside them. But don't let their size fool you. Microbes are capable of an incredible range of metabolic processes that are essential to life as we know it.

Let's dive deeper into the fascinating world of microbial energy production!

As we mentioned before, microbes have a range of ways to generate the energy they need to survive and thrive. Let's start with photosynthesis, a process often associated with plants but also used by some microbes.

Photosynthesis is a process that converts sunlight into energy. In this process, microbes use unique pigments called chlorophyll to capture energy from the sun and convert it into chemical energy. This chemical energy is then used to fuel the microbe's metabolic processes. Cyanobacteria, typically found in aquatic environments, can produce oxygen through their photosynthetic mechanism.

On the other hand, some microbes use organic compounds, such as glucose or other sugars, to produce energy through respiration. Respiration involves a series of chemical reactions that break down organic molecules, such as glucose, to release energy. One example of a microbe that uses respiration is the Escherichia coli (E. coli) bacteria, which is commonly found in the gut of humans and other animals.

And still, other microbes use inorganic compounds, such as sulfur or iron, to generate energy through chemosynthesis. Chemosynthesis is a process that uses the energy from chemical reactions to produce energy-rich molecules that can be used by the microbe. One example of a microbe that uses chemosynthesis is the deep-sea vent bacteria in the hot, acidic waters around deep-sea hydrothermal vents.

So, as you can see, microbes have a range of ways to generate the energy they need to survive and thrive. Microbes can power their metabolic processes and carry out essential life functions using sunlight, organic compounds, or inorganic compounds. This is just one example of the fantastic world of microbial metabolism and growth.

Now that we've explored energy production let's talk about how microbes acquire and process carbon and nitrogen. These two elements are crucial for life, and microbes have developed a range of metabolic pathways to acquire and process them.

Carbon is essential to organic molecules like carbohydrates, lipids, and proteins. Microbes use a process called carbon metabolism to acquire and process carbon. One example of carbon metabolism is the famous Calvin cycle used in photosynthesis, which we discussed earlier. This process involves using carbon dioxide from the air to build organic molecules, such as glucose, which can be used for energy or as building blocks for other molecules.

Nitrogen is another essential element for life, as it's needed to make amino acids and nucleotides. However, nitrogen in the atmosphere is in a form that living organisms can't use. Microbes have developed a process called the nitrogen cycle to convert atmospheric nitrogen into a form that can be used by living organisms. This process involves a series of chemical reactions that convert nitrogen gas into ammonium, which can then be used to make organic molecules.

Now, let's talk about fermentation. This metabolic process is used by some microbes to produce energy without the use of oxygen. Fermentation also produces many delicious foods and beverages, such as bread, beer, and yogurt. Microbes break down organic molecules, such as glucose, during fermentation to produce energy and other products like alcohol or lactic acid. One example of a microbe that uses fermentation is the yeast used to make bread and beer. When yeast is added to dough or wort, it ferments the sugars in the mixture, producing carbon dioxide gas that causes the dough to rise or the beer to become carbonated.

So, as you can see, microbes have a range of metabolic pathways to acquire and process essential nutrients like carbon and nitrogen. And fermentation is just one of the many fascinating ways microbes can produce energy and other products. Understanding microbial metabolism and growth is essential for understanding the role of microbes in the environment and our lives.

Of course, these metabolic processes are only possible if the microbes can grow and reproduce. Bacterial growth can be broken down into four distinct phases, each with its own characteristics. During the lag phase, bacteria are not yet growing but preparing to divide and multiply. This phase can last for a few hours or even days, depending on the type of microbe and its environment.

In the exponential phase, bacteria are growing and dividing exponentially. This means that their population doubles with each generation. If a single bacterium can grow in ideal conditions, it can produce over a billion bacteria in just 24 hours!

During the stationary phase, the growth rate slows, and the bacteria run out of resources. The stationary phase can last long as the bacteria balance growth and death. Eventually, during the death phase, the bacteria can no longer grow and reproduce, and their numbers begin to decline.

Factors such as temperature, pH, and nutrient availability can significantly impact microbial growth. For example, some bacteria prefer warmer temperatures, while others prefer cooler temperatures. pH is also essential, as some bacteria thrive in acidic environments, while others prefer alkaline environments. Nutrient availability is another crucial factor, as bacteria need a steady supply of nutrients to grow and reproduce.

Understanding these factors is essential for scientists who work with microbes in research, medicine, and industry. For example, microbiologists who work in the food industry need to understand the conditions that promote bacterial growth and take steps to prevent the growth of harmful bacteria in food products. Medical researchers also need to understand the factors that promote bacterial growth to develop effective treatments for bacterial infections.

Understanding microbial growth and reproduction is essential for understanding the role of microbes in our lives and the environment. Studying these fascinating microorganisms allows us to learn more about the world and develop new technologies to improve our lives.

So there you have a brief overview of microbial metabolism and growth. These tiny organisms might be small, but they play a significant role in the world around us. From producing the oxygen we breathe to breaking down organic matter in the soil, microbes are essential to life on Earth.

Microbial Genetics and Genetic Engineering

Hey there, future scientists! This chapter will dive into the fascinating world of microbial genetics and genetic engineering. Trust me, this is going to be an exciting ride!

So, what is microbial genetics exactly? Simply put, it's the study of the genetic material of microorganisms - tiny living organisms that are too small to see with the naked eye. These include bacteria, viruses, fungi, and other small creatures surrounding us daily.

Now, let's talk about one of the most exciting aspects of microbial genetics - gene expression. This is the process by which a gene's instructions are used to make a protein. Think of it like a recipe - the gene is the recipe, and the protein is the finished dish. Gene expression allows microorganisms to perform incredible functions, from breaking down food to defending against harmful invaders.

Let's take the example of bacteria that live in our gut. These bacteria play a crucial role in digesting the food we eat. When we eat, bacteria use their genes to produce enzymes that break down complex molecules into simpler ones that our bodies can absorb. Without these bacteria, we wouldn't be able to digest many of the foods we eat.

Another fascinating example of gene expression is in viruses. Did you know that viruses hijack the gene expression machinery of their host cells to replicate themselves? That's right! They use the host cell's genetic material to make copies of their own genetic material assembled into new viruses.

So, why is the study of microbial genetics so important? Understanding gene expression in microorganisms can help us develop new treatments for diseases caused by bacteria and viruses. For instance, by studying how bacteria use their genes to defend against antibiotics, we can develop new antibiotics to overcome their defenses.

Microbial genetics is a fascinating field that has the potential to revolutionize our understanding of the world around us. From bacteria in our gut to viruses that cause diseases, understanding how these tiny creatures use their genes to carry out incredible functions is vital to unlocking their secrets. I hope this chapter has piqued your interest and inspired you to learn more about this exciting field of science.

Now, let's delve deeper into the fascinating gene regulation and genetic recombination world.

So, as we know, DNA contains the instructions for making proteins, but it needs to be "read" to do so. This is where gene regulation comes in. Gene regulation is the process by which a cell controls which genes are turned on and off at any given time. Think of it like a light switch - some genes are turned on, while others are turned off. This allows microorganisms to adapt to their environment by producing only the needed proteins at any given time.

Let's take the example of bacteria that live in the soil. These bacteria are exposed to a wide range of nutrients and need to adapt to survive. So, when a specific nutrient is present, the bacteria will turn on the genes that allow them to break down that nutrient and use it for energy. When the nutrient is absent, the bacteria will turn off those genes and conserve energy until the next nutrient becomes available.

Now, let's talk about genetic recombination. This is the process by which genetic material is shuffled and swapped between different microorganisms. It's like a genetic game of mix and match! Genetic recombination allows microorganisms to evolve and adapt to their environment over time.

One example of genetic recombination is the transfer of antibiotic resistance genes between bacteria. This is a significant problem in modern medicine, making treating bacterial infections much harder. Antibiotic resistance genes can be transferred between bacteria through horizontal gene transfer, where genetic material is passed from one bacterium to another.

Another example of genetic recombination is viral reassortment. This process occurs when two different virus strains infect the same host cell. The genetic material of the two viruses can mix and match, creating a new strain with a unique combination of genes. This is how new strains of the flu virus emerge each year.

In conclusion, gene regulation and recombination are essential microbial genetic processes. These processes allow microorganisms to adapt and evolve, making them incredibly resilient and versatile. I hope this chapter has helped you understand these concepts better and inspired you to learn more about microbial genetics.

In the previous section, we discussed gene regulation and genetic recombination. Now, let's talk about the fascinating stuff - genetic engineering!

Genetic engineering is the process by which scientists can manipulate the genetic material of an organism to give it new traits or abilities. This can potentially revolutionize many fields, from medicine to agriculture and even conservation.

One of the most common techniques used in genetic engineering is gene cloning. This involves copying a gene and inserting it into another organism, where it can be expressed and used to produce a desired protein. For example, scientists can clone the gene that codes for insulin and insert it into bacteria, which can then produce large quantities of insulin for treating diabetes.

Another technique that's been gaining a lot of attention is CRISPR/Cas9. This is a powerful tool that allows scientists to precisely edit DNA. It uses a "guide RNA" to direct an enzyme called Cas9 to a specific location in the DNA. Once there, Cas9 can cut the DNA and insert, delete, or replace specific pieces of genetic material. This has the potential to cure genetic diseases, create crops that are more resistant to pests and diseases, and even bring extinct species back to life!

One example of genetic engineering in action is the creation of genetically modified crops. Scientists can use genetic engineering techniques to introduce new traits into crops, such as resistance to pests or tolerance to drought. This can potentially increase crop yields and help feed a growing global population.

Another example is the development of gene therapies for genetic diseases. Scientists can use gene editing techniques like CRISPR/Cas9 to correct the underlying genetic mutations that cause sickle cell anemia and cystic fibrosis. This can potentially cure these diseases rather than treat the symptoms.

With genetic engineering, the possibilities are endless. Scientists are utilizing it to generate new medications, resistant crops to pests and illnesses, and even bring extinct creatures back to life (yep, you read that correctly!).

So, there you have it - a brief overview of microbial genetics and genetic engineering. Who knew that such tiny organisms could hold so much power and potential? The more we learn about microbial genetics, the more we can harness that power and use it to improve the world.

So go forth, young scientists, and discover the secrets of the microbe world!

Pathogenic Microbes and Host-Pathogen Interactions

As we go about our daily lives, we encounter a variety of microorganisms. Some are harmless, while others can cause severe illness. This chapter will explore the fascinating world of pathogenic microbes and their interactions with the human body.

At their core, infectious diseases are caused by microorganisms that invade the body and cause harm. These tiny organisms, such as bacteria, viruses, fungi, and parasites, are called pathogens. While small, they can wreak havoc on the body's tissues and organs, leading to severe illness or even death.

Let's dive a little deeper into how pathogens can enter the body and how our immune system works to defend against them.

One way that pathogens can enter the body is through the air we breathe. For example, when someone with the flu coughs or sneezes, tiny droplets containing the virus can be spread into the air and inhaled by others nearby. Another way that pathogens can enter the body is through contaminated food or water. For instance, drinking water contaminated with a parasite like Giardia can lead to a severe stomach illness.

Once inside the body, pathogens can use their unique characteristics to replicate and spread throughout the body, causing harm to the host's tissues. For instance, the bacterium *Streptococcus pyogenes*, which causes strep throat, produces a toxin that can damage the throat and other tissues.

Fortunately, our immune system can recognize and fight these foreign invaders. When a pathogen enters the body, the immune system produces antibodies and other defence mechanisms to neutralize the threat. Antibodies are like little soldiers that target specific pathogens and help to neutralize them.

For example, when someone is infected with the chickenpox virus, their immune system produces antibodies explicitly targeting it. These antibodies help to neutralize the virus, preventing it from replicating and spreading throughout the body. Over time, the body builds up immunity to the virus, making it less likely to cause harm in the future.

However, pathogens are not easily defeated. They have evolved various strategies to evade the host's defences and continue to cause damage. For example, some bacteria can produce enzymes that destroy antibodies. In contrast, others can alter their surface proteins to evade detection by the immune system. It's a constant battle between our immune system and the pathogens that seek to harm us.

Understanding how pathogens enter the body and how our immune system defends against them is essential to staying healthy. By preventing the spread of pathogens, such as washing our hands and getting vaccinated, we can help protect ourselves and others from harm. And by supporting research into new treatments and vaccines, we can continue to improve our ability to fight off infectious diseases.

It's true that pathogens are very clever and have evolved to sneak past our immune system's defences. For example, some bacteria have developed the ability to produce enzymes that destroy the antibodies that our immune system produces to fight them off. This makes it much harder for our bodies to fight off the infection.

Other pathogens can alter their surface proteins to make themselves look different to our immune system. This is like wearing a disguise, so the immune system doesn't recognize them as a threat. By doing this, they can avoid being attacked by our immune system and continue to cause harm to our bodies.

But don't worry. Scientists are always working hard to develop new ways to prevent and treat infectious diseases. By studying how these tiny organisms work and interact with our bodies, we can develop new vaccines and treatments to protect against them.

For example, when scientists discovered that some bacteria produce enzymes to destroy antibodies, they started looking for ways to block them. Doing this could help our immune system's antibodies do their job and fight off the infection.

Another strategy that scientists are exploring is developing vaccines that target different parts of the pathogen. By doing this, they can train our immune system to recognize and fight off the pathogen, even if it tries to change its surface proteins.

While pathogens can be tricky to fight off, new strategies are constantly being developed to keep us healthy. By learning more about these tiny organisms and their interactions with our bodies, we can stay one step ahead and protect ourselves and others from infectious diseases.

The study of pathogenic microbes and host-pathogen interactions is a fascinating and critical area of research. By delving into this topic, we can better understand how infectious diseases spread and develop new ways to protect ourselves from harm. Whether you're a high school student interested in biology or a curious reader, there's something to learn from the world of pathogenic microbes.

Microbial Ecology and Environmental Microbiology

Hey there, dear readers! Are you ready to join us in exploring the fascinating world of microbes and their environmental impact? This chapter will dive into the fantastic fields of microbial ecology and environmental microbiology. We'll learn about the interactions between microorganisms and their surroundings, their vital roles in nutrient cycling and biogeochemical cycles, and the methods used to study microbial ecology. So, grab your microscope, and let's get started on this thrilling adventure!

Microbial ecology is the study of how microorganisms interact with their environment. Microbes are everywhere, from the soil beneath our feet to the depths of the oceans. They play crucial roles in biogeochemical cycles, which are the pathways that elements like carbon, nitrogen, and phosphorus take through the environment.

Let's dive deeper into microbes' unique roles in our environment.

One of the most essential things that microbes do is nutrient cycling. Imagine a world without microbes to break down dead plant and animal matter. The world would be overrun with debris, and the nutrients locked within it would not be accessible to other living organisms. Microbes break down this organic matter, recycling its nutrients into the ecosystem. For example, when a leaf falls off a tree, microbes break down the leaf, freeing up the nutrients within it. Those nutrients are then available for other organisms, like the tree, to use to grow and thrive.

Microbes also form symbiotic relationships with other organisms. A great example of a beneficial relationship is the one between leguminous plants and nitrogen-fixing bacteria. These bacteria live on the roots of leguminous plants, like beans and peas, and they help the plants to grow. The bacteria take nitrogen from the air and convert it into a form the plant can use for growth. In return, the bacteria get home and food from the plant. This is an example of a win-win situation where both the plant and the bacteria benefit.

On the other hand, some microbial relationships can be harmful, like the ones between pathogens and humans or animals. Pathogens are microbes that cause disease. For example, the bacterium that causes tuberculosis is a pathogen. It spreads from person to person through the air and can cause serious illness. Understanding the relationships between microbes and their hosts is critical to preventing and treating diseases.

Microbes play crucial roles in our environment. They recycle nutrients, form beneficial relationships with other organisms, and even cause harm in some cases. By studying microbial ecology and environmental microbiology, we can gain a better understanding of how these tiny organisms impact our world and find ways to work with them to create a healthier planet.

Studying microbial ecology is no easy feat. In this section, we will explore scientists' methods to study microbes and how environmental microbiology can help solve real-world problems.

Studying microbes can be challenging because they are incredibly diverse and complex and live in many different environments. However, scientists have developed a range of techniques to study these tiny organisms. One method is DNA sequencing, which allows scientists to identify the different types of microbes present in a sample. Microscopy is another technique that scientists use to observe the structures of microbes. Finally, culturing allows scientists to grow microbes in a lab to study their behavior and characteristics. These techniques allow scientists to learn more about microbes' role in our environment.

Environmental microbiology is the application of microbial ecology to real-world problems. For example, scientists use microbes to clean up the environmental pollution. When an oil spill happens in the ocean, it can be devastating to marine life. However, some microbes can break down the oil into less harmful substances. Scientists can introduce these microbes into the affected area to speed up the cleanup process and reduce environmental damage.

In agriculture, microbes are used to improve soil quality and plant growth. Farmers can add certain microbes to the soil to help break down organic matter and release nutrients. This makes the soil more fertile and reduces the need for harmful fertilizers and pesticides. In this way, microbes can help us grow food more sustainably and protect the environment at the same time.

Studying microbes is a complex but rewarding field of study. With techniques like DNA sequencing, microscopy, and culturing, scientists can learn more about these tiny organisms and their role in our environment. By applying this knowledge to real-world problems through environmental microbiology, we can use microbes to create a healthier and more sustainable planet.

Microbial ecology and environmental microbiology are significant fields of study. Microbes may be tiny, but their impact on our planet is enormous. By studying these tiny organisms, we can better understand how our world works and find ways to work with nature instead of against it.

Thanks for reading, and stay curious!

Biotechnology and Microbial Applications

As we move towards a more sustainable future, it's becoming increasingly clear that microorganisms have an essential role in biotechnology. From fermentation to bioremediation and the production of biopharmaceuticals, these tiny organisms offer a world of possibilities that we are only beginning to explore.

Let's look at the fascinating world of microbial fermentation and how it's used to create some of our favourite foods.

As you may already know, fermentation is a process that involves the breakdown of sugars by microorganisms like bacteria and fungi. This process releases energy and produces a range of by products, including acids, gases, and alcohol.

One of the most well-known examples of microbial fermentation is bread production. When yeast is added to bread dough, it feeds on the sugars in the flour, producing carbon dioxide gas. This gas causes the dough to rise, resulting in the fluffy texture we associate with bread.

But did you know that many other delicious foods are also made using microbial fermentation? Yogurt, for example, is made by adding specific bacteria to milk. These bacteria feed on the lactose in the milk, producing lactic acid and causing the milk to thicken and develop its characteristic tangy flavour.

Cheese is another popular food that is made using microbial fermentation. In this case, bacteria or fungi are added to milk to create curds. These curds are pressed, drained, and aged to produce various kinds of cheese with unique flavours and textures.

You might be familiar with other fermented foods, including pickles, sauerkraut, and kimchi. Each of these foods uses specific strains of bacteria that break down the sugars in vegetables, resulting in their distinctive flavours and textures.

In addition to being delicious, fermented foods also offer a range of health benefits. They are a great source of probiotics, beneficial bacteria that can help support digestive health and boost the immune system.

So, the next time you enjoy a slice of bread or a bowl of yogurt, remember that microbial fermentation is behind the unique flavours and textures that make these foods special. And if you're feeling adventurous, why not try making your own fermented foods at home? With a little bit of experimentation, you might discover a new favourite dish!

Bioremediation, on the other hand, involves using microorganisms to clean up environmental pollution. Bioremediation is a process that involves using microorganisms like bacteria to break down harmful chemicals and pollutants in the environment. For example, some bacteria can break down oil into simpler, harmless compounds. This makes them extremely valuable in cleaning up oil spills and other environmental disasters.

One famous example of bioremediation is the clean-up of the Exxon Valdez oil spill in Alaska in 1989. In this disaster, an oil tanker ran aground. It spilled millions of gallons of oil into the ocean, causing widespread damage to the environment and local wildlife.

To clean up the spill, researchers introduced a type of bacteria called *Alcanivorax borkumensis*. These bacteria can break down hydrocarbons, the main component of crude oil, into simpler compounds that are harmless to the environment. Over time, the bacteria reduced the amount of oil in the water, allowing the ecosystem to recover.

But bioremediation isn't just helpful in cleaning up oil spills. It's also being used to combat other types of pollution, such as chemical spills and industrial waste. By harnessing the power of microorganisms, we can turn harmful pollutants into harmless substances, protecting both the environment and human health.

In fact, bioremediation is becoming an increasingly important tool in the fight against climate change. By breaking down harmful greenhouse gases like methane and carbon dioxide, microorganisms could help us reduce our carbon footprint and mitigate the effects of climate change.

So, the next time you hear about a pollution disaster or worry about the impact of climate change, remember that bioremediation and the power of microorganisms could be part of the solution. And who knows, maybe one day you'll be the scientist or engineer who discovers the next breakthrough in this exciting field!

Finally, microorganisms also produce biopharmaceuticals - drugs derived from biological sources. These medicines have revolutionized the field of medicine, helping to treat and cure a wide range of diseases, from cancer to diabetes.

But did you know that many of these drugs are produced using microorganisms? That's right - bacteria, yeast, and other microbes are used to manufacture these medicines in a process called biotechnology.

One example of a biopharmaceutical produced using microorganisms is insulin. This hormone is essential for regulating blood sugar levels in people with diabetes. Previously, insulin was extracted from the pancreas of animals such as pigs and cows, which was costly and frequently resulted in medicine shortages.

Thanks to biotechnology, insulin can be produced more efficiently and sustainably using genetically engineered bacteria such as Escherichia coli or yeast. These microbes can produce human insulin, which is identical to the insulin produced by our own bodies, at a much lower cost.

Another example of a biopharmaceutical produced using microorganisms is the hepatitis B vaccine, which helps protect against potentially life-threatening liver disease. The vaccine is made using yeast that has been genetically modified to produce a protein found in the hepatitis B virus. This protein triggers an immune response in the body, helping to protect against the virus.

By using microorganisms to produce biopharmaceuticals, we can ensure that these lifesaving medicines are accessible to people worldwide. Biotechnology has made it possible to produce these drugs more efficiently, which means they can be produced at a lower cost and in larger quantities.

So, the next time you take a lifesaving medicine, remember that microorganisms and biotechnology could be behind its production. Who knows, maybe one day you'll be the scientist or engineer who discovers the next breakthrough in this exciting field!

But as with any technology, there are also ethical considerations to take into account. Using microorganisms in biotechnology raises questions about safety, regulation, and the potential unintended consequences of our actions. As we continue to explore the possibilities of this field, we must do so responsibly and thoughtfully, considering the impact on human health and the environment.

The applications of microorganisms in biotechnology are vast and varied, offering us new ways to produce food, clean up pollution, and improve human health. But as with any powerful technology, we must approach it with care and consideration, ensuring that we use it to benefit both people and the planet.

Microbiology and Society

Welcome to the final chapter of our journey through the fascinating world of microbiology! We've explored the tiny creatures that make up our world and their incredible impact on our daily lives. In this chapter, we'll look at the broader implications of microbiology in society.

Microbes play a vital role in human health, agriculture, and industry. They help us digest food, produce medicines, and even clean up oil spills! In fact, without microbes, life as we know it wouldn't exist. But with great power comes great responsibility. We must be aware of the social and ethical implications of microbiology, such as the impact of microbial biotechnology on the environment and the use of antibiotics in medicine.

Let's take a closer look at how microbiology affects our health.

Firstly, microbes can cause disease. You've probably heard of bacteria like E. coli and Salmonella, which can make you sick if you eat contaminated food. Or viruses like the flu and COVID-19 can spread through the air and cause respiratory illness. But did you know that some bacteria are actually good for us? Our gut microbiome, the collection of bacteria in our intestines, helps us digest food and boosts our immune system. In fact, some studies have even shown that the gut microbiome can impact our mental health!

However, microbes can also be our enemies. Antibiotic resistance is a growing problem where bacteria become immune to the drugs we use to treat them. This can make even superficial infections challenging to treat, leading to more severe illnesses. For example, suppose you get an infection from a cut on your hand. In that case, a doctor might prescribe antibiotics to help fight the bacteria. But if those bacteria are resistant to the antibiotics, the infection can spread and become more dangerous.

So, what can we do about antibiotic resistance? Firstly, we need to use antibiotics responsibly. Only take antibiotics when needed and ensure you finish the entire course, even if you start feeling better. This will help prevent the development of antibiotic-resistant bacteria. We also need to find new ways to treat infections. Scientists are developing new antibiotics and other treatments, such as using bacteriophages, viruses that attack bacteria, to fight infections.

Did you know that microbes can be our allies when growing crops? Some microbes, like bacteria and fungi, help plants grow by fixing nitrogen in the soil and breaking down organic matter. This makes nutrients available to the plants and helps them grow strong and healthy. Some microbes can even form symbiotic relationships with plant roots, exchanging nutrients for sugars in a process called mycorrhization.

Microbes can also be used to control pests in a biological pest control process. Certain bacteria and fungi can infect and kill pests without harming the plants. This reduces the need for chemical pesticides, which can harm the environment and human health. Using microbes for pest control is a sustainable alternative that benefits both the plants and the ecosystem.

However, we must be careful when using microbiology in agriculture. For example, genetically modified crops have been designed to resist pests and diseases by inserting genes from other organisms. While this can increase crop yields and reduce the need for pesticides, it can also have unintended consequences on the ecosystem. For example, suppose a genetically modified crop produces a toxin that kills pests. In that case, it could also harm other beneficial insects, like bees, that are important for pollination.

Let's talk about how microbiology impacts the industry.

Did you know that microbes are used to produce many of the products we use every day? For example, certain bacteria are used to make cheese, yogurt, and other dairy products. Yeast is used to make bread, beer, and wine. And some types of bacteria can even produce biofuels and plastics!

Microbial biotechnology is a rapidly growing field that has the potential to revolutionize the industry. By engineering microbes to produce specific compounds, we can create new and innovative products that are more sustainable and eco-friendly. For example, scientists are researching ways to use microbes to break down plastic waste and create biodegradable materials.

However, we must be careful when using microbial biotechnology in industry. For example, if genetically modified microbes are released into the wild, they could have unforeseen consequences on the ecosystem. That's why conducting thorough research and risk assessments is vital before using microbial biotechnology in the industry.

As we can see, microbiology has far-reaching implications for society. We must use this knowledge responsibly and make informed decisions about using microbes to benefit ourselves and the planet. By working together, we can harness the power of microbiology to create a better, healthier, and more sustainable world for everyone.

Final Words

Congratulations, you have completed our journey through the fascinating world of microbiology! Throughout this book, you have explored the diverse and complex world of microorganisms, including bacteria, archaea, fungi, protists, and viruses. You have learned about their roles in the environment and human health, their metabolism, genetics, and diversity, and their applications in biotechnology.

As you have seen, microbiology is an exciting and rapidly evolving field of study with countless opportunities for discovery and innovation. Advances in technology and research have revolutionized our understanding of the microbial world, leading to breakthroughs in medicine, biotechnology, and environmental science.

One of the most exciting study fields in microbiology is the development of innovative antimicrobial medications to tackle infectious diseases. Scientists are working tirelessly to develop new drugs and therapies that can target and kill harmful microbes while leaving the beneficial ones intact. This research is critical in the fight against antibiotic-resistant bacteria, which pose a growing threat to public health.

Another area of research with tremendous potential is using microorganisms in biotechnology. Microbes produce a wide range of products, from food and fuel to pharmaceuticals and industrial chemicals. This research can transform our society by reducing our dependence on fossil fuels and promoting sustainable practices.

As you have seen throughout this book, microbiology is incredibly diverse, with countless applications and implications. The study of microorganisms has the potential to revolutionize our understanding of the world and improve our lives in countless ways. Whether you are interested in medicine, biotechnology, or environmental science, microbiology offers endless opportunities for discovery and innovation.

So, as you progress in your studies and career, remember the fascinating world of microbiology and the countless opportunities it presents. Who knows, you may be the one to make the subsequent breakthrough discovery!

About the Authors

Dr. Anjana J.C. holds a Ph.D. in Medical Microbiology from Bharathiar University. She is a highly accomplished microbiology educator and researcher with over a decade of experience.

Dr. Anjana is an expert in making complex concepts simple and engaging. With her confident and articulate communication skills, she can convey even the most intricate ideas in a clear and concise manner, making it easy for students to understand and excel in their studies.

With her passion, expertise, and commitment to excellence, Dr. Anjana is a force to be reckoned with in the world of microbiology education and research.

Sanath Nair is a seasoned sales and marketing professional with over 2 decades of experience in the industry. With his Bachelor of Engineering in Production and Master's degree in International Business, he has worked with some great teams and companies.

In his free time, he channels his creativity through writing and maintains a personal blog called Fresher Blog. He shares his thoughts and insights on various topics through his blog, showcasing his love for the written word.

Visit the blog here: -

Made in the USA
Las Vegas, NV
04 January 2025

15881161R00026